To J.
From NaNa Narleen/
.

PULL OFF YOUR DREAM!

DR. THOMASINA A. JONES

PUBLISHED BY INFINITY PUBLISHING

PULL OFF YOUR DREAM!

First Edition

Print edition ISBN: 9781499904048

Library of Congress Control Number: 2018936067

Printed in the United States of America

TABLE OF CONTENTS

DEDICATION

To all of the high school seniors who shared
their dreams with me, stay the course, until
you accomplish and pull of your dreams!

Acknowledgments

I am grateful and obliged to all of the high school seniors who merrily and readily shared their dreams with me. Each one of you propelled me to write Pull Off Your Dream!

I am grateful to my Lord and Savior Jesus Christ for all of the bountiful blessings that He has bestowed upon me! I am fortunate to have a supportive husband, magnificent parents, amazing children, siblings, and a host of wonderful relatives and friends who promoted and fostered my dreams! They continue to cultivate and nurture my dreams as I embark upon pulling off my most recent dream. I am currently enrolled in a prestigious seminary where I will obtain my M.A. in Christian Leadership! I am indebted to everyone who sponsors me along my breathtaking journey.

Introduction

<u>D</u>esire, <u>R</u>each, <u>E</u>mbrace, <u>A</u>ction,
<u>M</u>anifestation!

The awe-inspiring, incredible, and phenomenal Ms. Viola Davis delivered an arousing, cogent, and powerful acceptance speech when she won her first Oscar for Best Supporting Actress in *Fences*. The marvelous and sensational Viola Davis stated the following during her acceptance speech, "Thank you to the Academy. You know, there's one place that all the people with the greatest potential are gathered. One place and that's the graveyard. People ask me all the time, what kind of stories do you want to tell, Viola? And I say, exhume those bodies. Exhume those stories. The stories of the people who dreamed big and never saw those dreams to fruition."

There are a myriad of people who are living and those who are housed in cemeteries with unfulfilled dreams. Scores of people had an idea, vision, mental image and mental picture of a dream that they want to or wanted to achieve. It is extremely disheartening to know that there are countless gifted and talented people in the world who have dreams or had dreams that never materialized. It is incumbent upon every man, woman, boy and girl to be on a relentless pursuit to accomplish their dreams while they have the ability, stamina, strength, and health and wellness to attain their goals.

There would be no need to unearth the bodies of people who had the potential to accomplish their dreams if folks could attain their dreams, and live to tell their own stories. It is time to behold and conceptualize the goal that you have been carrying in the crevices of your heart for a prolonged period. It is time to pull off your dream!

Pull Off Your Dream will catapult and propel you to attain and procure your dream. It is my hope that this book will encourage you to activate and manifest the dream that is planted in the essence of your soul. As long as you have courage, fortitude, tenacity, vigor and vitality, it is never too late to fulfill your dream!

CHAPTER ONE

A Dream Emanates with a DESIRE!

There are conversations that occur in homes, classrooms, places of worship, around campfires, at kitchen tables, barbershops, hair salons, gyms, coffee bars, restaurants, fraternities, sororities, on airplanes, and in cars where people huddle and gather to share their ambitions, dreams, passions, and desires. All dreams emit from a strong hunger, thirst, panting and yearning desire to accomplish a goal and purpose. Absent a desire, there is no dream! A dream emanates with a desire!

The people who crave for, long for, want and desire to attain their aspirations, goals and dreams generally share the desires that are in the crux of their hearts with people who surround them. They are not ambivalent or reticent to share the dreams they crave for, long for, want and desire to pull off along the journey.

We have at one time or another been captivated by someone sharing their passions with us. The people who share their desires with us create a mental image of their goals for us to comprehend. They are so passionate and zealous when they share their parables that we undoubtedly believe they will pull off their dreams!

I, like many of you, have heard litanies of people emotionally and fervently declare and proclaim their heartfelt desires over the years. I have been engrossed and caught up in conversations with students in classrooms, colleagues at work, and parishioners at church, family members, friends and strangers who have shared their heartfelt desires with me. They shared their hopes and dreams with such fervor, infatuation, and enthusiasm that I was convinced their dreams would come to fulfillment!

Unfortunately, I have found that many of the people who enthralled me with their desires to obtain their dreams did not pull off their dreams. They were cemented in the desire stage and never moved from having colloquy, dialogue, and deliberation to launching the work that was necessary for them to achieve their goals.

I have attended a multitude of middle and high school career-day festivities. There were students who shared their aspirations and ambitions with me. I was always captivated and mesmerized by the number of students who immediately informed me that they desired to serve as attorneys, teachers, medical doctors, engineers, veterinarians, forensic scientists, military personnel, nurses, computer scientists, and star athletes when questioned about their career aspirations. The students would share their desires with such enthusiasm and excitement that I would be fired up and inspired because I thought so many students were on track to obtain their dreams. Upon questioning the students regarding their program of studies, extracurricular activities, community service endeavors, hobbies, or participation in athletic and visual and performing arts activities, I found that some of the students were not participating in the essential undertakings, coursework, community service and extracurricular activities, or athletic and visual and performing arts activities that would enable them to accomplish their dreams. The students, like thousands of other dream bearers, were stuck in the desire stage.

We all know people who will enthrall us in confabulation about their dreams. The people will share stories about their desire to lose weight, enroll in graduate school, attend trade school, open a restaurant, launch a business, write a book or script for a sitcom, record a song, change the plight of the homeless, run for a political office, change careers, obtain a college degree, become a homeowner, or take a trip to Africa or Europe. The people will share their scripts, never digressing from them, because in their hearts and minds they see the mental image of themselves accomplishing their desires. The dilemma is that every dream emanates with a desire; however, in order for people to pull off their dreams, they must not only converse about their dreams, they also have to reach for their dreams!

CHAPTER TWO

You Must REACH for Your Dream!

There are scores of people who have a burning desire to carry out their dreams, but fear has immobilized them from actualizing their dreams. I heard someone give an acronym for the word "fear." The acronym is: false evidence appearing real! There are people who are grounded in the desire stage because they have become incapacitated and paralyzed by fear and all of the false, outlandish, bogus and invalid reasons for not realizing their dreams.

There are people, institutions, organizations, family and friends who have planted fear in the hearts of people that has caused them to abandon their dreams.

It is incumbent upon you to eradicate and blot out the false evidence that appears to be real if you are going to pull off your dream. The spirit of fear will overtake and extinguish your dream!

It is essential to maintain the belief and confidence that your dream is reachable. You must maintain the momentum to carry out your dream by arousing and inciting the desire to reach for your dream!

There are countless people who are in cemeteries because they did not move from desire to the ability to reach for their dreams. It is incumbent upon all dream bearers to examine and scrutinize the scope of their dreams. It is not enough to just have a mental image of who you want to become or what you want to do in life. It is essential that you approach, get a hold of, and appraise every element of your dream. You have to make contact with the tenets you will need to reach and seize your dream.

Dream bearers reach for their goals by assessing the terrain and getting in touch with the components, people, resources, and variables needed to realize their dreams. They look for the opportunity to seize or attain their goals by recognizing that there is some research involved to attain their goals. People who reach for their dreams also understand they must build capacity in themselves if they want to be empowered to execute their dreams.

I have been fortunate enough to have the same hairstylist for the past fifteen years. I noticed the young skilled, talented cosmetologist when I stopped by a nationwide hair salon to purchase some hair products. I immediately noticed that her chair was located at the back of the salon. I observed that every time I visited the salon, she was always servicing a client. Most of the hairstylists did not appear to have an astronomic number of clientele. I often observed their vacant chairs while the hairstylist in the back always had an occupied chair. I later uncovered that she requested to have her chair in the back of the salon to create a private area for her clients.

One day, I asked the accomplished hairstylist if she had any availability on her schedule to wash, blow-dry, and flat-iron my hair. She had such an exhaustive list of clients that I had to wait at least eight to twelve weeks to obtain an appointment! She was so active servicing clients that she yielded more capital than any other cosmetologist in the entire salon!

I was finally able to receive (after a couple of years) a fixed every-other-Friday appointment with my hairstylist. I noticed that after we developed a relationship, she would share her dream with me. She had longed and craved for her own hair salon. She would passionately chat about her aspiration and fire to open her own hair salon.

One Friday, she informed me that she had embarked upon the research to open her own hair salon. She realized it was not enough just to desire to have her own business. She needed to approach and reach for her dream by learning the intricacies of entrepreneurship.

She reached for her dream by enrolling in business classes offered at a local community action agency. She was adamant she wanted to enlist in classes to learn the business landscape. She attained and seized the opportunity to acquire knowledge and wisdom in the business realm in order to be a successful entrepreneur.

Today, my cosmetologist of twenty years is a successful entrepreneur who owns a hair salon because she reached for her dream. She has been able to build such an extensive list of clients that the only way she can service a new client is if one of her longstanding clients has a scheduling conflict.

We all know people who shared their dreams with us along the journey. There are people who never moved from discourse to reaching for or subscribing to their dreams. After a while, the people who are passionate about their desires and never reach for their dreams are in jeopardy of aborting their dreams because they are cemented in the desire stage too long. It is not enough to be mesmerized about a dream. Everyone who has successfully attained their goals reached for their dreams.

I want you to stop and reflect upon a dream that you had once upon a time. What caused you to scrap the dream? Did you have an insurmountable amount of fear that disabled you?

Did you blame it on your age, lack of opportunities, people, family issues, life experiences, adverse or catastrophic events, or lack of resources? I am not invalidating or nullifying the reasons why you believe that you terminated your dream. I do know that oftentimes, what causes dreams to erode and wane is that we don't invest the time and energy to reach for our dreams.

What dream has been deferred in your life? Are you enthusiastically conversing about your dream? Can you see a mental image of the dream? Are you reaching for your dream? Are you conducting all the essential research that will enable you to overtake your dream?

I encourage you to activate and pull off your dream. The burning and yearning desire is planted in your heart. Propel your dream by reaching for all information, tools, and resources you will need for your dream to materialize.

It is incumbent upon you to stop, grab a piece of paper, notebook, or journal, and pen or take out your electronic device and record the dream that has been burning in your heart for an extended period of time. I want you to read your vision every day. You will be less likely to abort your dream if you refer to the inscription regularly and wholeheartedly embrace your dream!

CHAPTER THREE

You Must EMBRACE Your Dream!

I had the privilege of talking to over two hundred high school graduating seniors during the month of June. I submitted a dream interest card to the seniors in May. I simply requested that the high school seniors complete the following sentence: "In ten years, my dream is to_____." The students filled in the blank. I was flabbergasted and pleasantly surprised by some of their responses.

They stated all of the dreams they wanted to accomplish in ten years. I recalled some of the students' dreams. I will share some of their dreams with you. In ten years, my dream is to become a veterinarian, doctor, attorney, forensic scientist, pediatrician, airplane pilot, military officer, a nurse, accountant, computer programmer, college professor, teacher, professional singer, actress, actor, a motivational speaker, pastor or to become wealthy.

My administrative assistant compiled all two hundred-plus students' dreams and uploaded the information into a PowerPoint to be shown to the students the day before the seniors began rehearsing for their graduation ceremony.

All the graduating seniors were invited to an assembly. The students had no inclination or idea that the assembly would be about them! The students observed a PowerPoint presentation of their high school classmates' graduation pictures and their dreams all while R. Kelly's "I Believe I Can Fly" music was playing in the background. I also shared their dreams with their peers, teachers, counselors, and itinerant staff.

I must say that it was a tearjerker for the students and staff. Some students chuckled at their peers' dreams because in their minds, their peers selected dreams they thought were unreachable.

The students departed the assembly realizing and recognizing that everyone was aware of their aspirations and dreams. They suddenly recognized that graduation was lurking around the corner and it was time to relentlessly pursue their dreams if they wanted to attain them in ten years!

Most of us may have been asked the same question I asked the students along the journey. Where do you see yourself ten years from now? Perhaps we, like the students, may have engraved and recorded our hopes and dreams in an electronic note page, journal, on a vision board, or on a simple piece of scrap paper with the hope that our dreams would come to fruition. We ardently believed that we had a lot of time to obtain our dreams because after all, ten years was a lot of time. Certainly anyone can possibly obtain their dreams if granted a ten-year timeline. Albeit time does not wait for anyone. Ten years is not a life span. We must seize every second, minute, and hour of the day to embrace and pull off our dreams!

Unfortunately, if we fail to embrace and hold close our dreams, our goals will come to naught. We must clutch and envelop our dreams if we want to accomplish our dreams.

I was one of the high school students who over thirty-eight years ago sat down and told my teachers and counselors my ten-year post-high school plans. I thought ten years was a lot of time because at the time, my aspiration was to be a teacher. It would only take me four to five years to achieve my bachelor's degree. Unfortunately, I faced an unanticipated life experience that immediately changed the trajectory of my life. The life experience was so colossal and monumental that I truly believed my dream had been terminated.

My plans to enroll at a college in Miami were suddenly adjourned. I found myself having to work at a menial job. The entire time I was employed in the factory, I never let go of my dream. I cultivated and nurtured my dream daily. My daydreams were permeated with a vision that was deferred. I could not blot out the dream that was burning in the nexus of my soul.

I was consumed and saturated with circumstances and events that could have caused me to let go of my dream. My untiring and steadfast faith in God gave me the ability to embrace my dream in spite of the conditions I faced at the plant.

I had to fight tooth and nail to clasp, clench, and hold on to my dream. I was surrounded by people who thought going to college was simply a pipe dream. There were people in the industrial unit who embraced the idea of working at a menial job, with low wages and poor health benefits. They were the people who would constantly encourage me to let go of my dream.

Fortunately, I met an incredible lady at the factory who also was bearing and carrying a dream in the bosom of her soul. She wanted to be a registered nurse. Her life experiences coupled with the rearing of her children caused her to delay her dream to become a registered nurse. The two of us would discuss our dreams to attend college while serving on the assembly line together. We encouraged each other to grip our dreams. We made a decision and covenant that we would egg on and support each other to pull off our dreams! We were not going to abort our dreams!

All while working at the factory, I encased myself in literature, contacted colleges for their program of studies, and immersed myself in any information that would keep me apprised of my dream. I really believed that embracing my dream was critical to actually fulfilling my dream. If I had abandoned my dream due to a life-changing event, discomfort, and the complexities of life, I would have yielded to defeat. Fortunately, my ability to clasp, cradle, and snuggle my dream in concert with prayer, grit, and tenacity and a lady in a factory who also had a dream allowed me to pull off my dream! I obtained my associate's degree followed by a bachelor's degree several years after I graduated from high school!

The lady who worked alongside me in the plant also pulled off her dream to become a registered nurse! We endorsed, promoted, and sponsored each other during the journey. We both held on to and embraced our dreams. I am ecstatic to report that today, the two of us remain close friends after serving over thirty-six years ago on an assembly line in an industrial plant!

Every June when I met with the graduating seniors, it was an emotional time for me because I realized that my students may encounter some life experiences and eventful circumstances that could cause them to let go of their dreams. It is critical for all dream bearers to realize that it is imperative to cling to, clinch, embrace, and grab hold of their dreams in spite of the challenges, life experiences, adverse situations, and catastrophic events they encounter along their odyssey.

I wish that you could coast and glide into accomplishing your dream. The truth of the matter is that in order to pull off your dream, you are going to experience some adversity, catastrophes, and opposition. You are going to have to battle, grapple, and wrestle to attain your dream. There is going to be blood, sweat, and tears involved in realizing your dream. You must gird yourself up for the barrage of things that will campaign against you to annul your dream.

Locate someone who will serve as an ally and encourage you to embrace and place a death grip on your dream like I did. The person will be your accountability partner. He or she will be there to edify and uplift you when you are contemplating discarding your dream.

Life-changing experiences will cause you to want to abort your dream. Your sponsor and devoted supporter will not allow you to concede, submit, yield or surrender to defeat!

You must earnestly fight to cradle your dream. Once you have embraced your dream, it should propel you to action. It will take action on your part to realize and pull off your dream!

CHAPTER FOUR

ACTION Is Required to Pull Off Your Dream!

There are hundreds of thousands of people who are carrying dreams that are in the embryonic stage. They have fondled and nursed the dream for years and in some cases decades. They have talked to an immeasurable number of people about their dreams and goals. They reached for their dreams by evaluating the terrain and researching the elements needed to accomplish their dreams. Unfortunately, their dreams are waiting to move from the embryonic stage at least to the gestational stage. The problem is that the dream has been dormant for so many years that the dream bearer does not have the confidence to activate and pull off the dream.

There are an incalculable number of people who have shared their dreams without embarking upon any action. People who listen to the folks consistently talk about their dreams with no action will eventually deem them as people who simply have pipe dreams. They will see them as folks who live in a fantasy world with unrealistic hopes and dreams. They have heard the precise accounts of the people who claim to be on the cusp of pulling off their dreams.

Dreams are not ever going to materialize by osmosis. The fulfillment of dreams requires action on the part of the dream bearers. Action means that you must do the work to consummate your dream! You must do something if you want to see your dream fulfilled.

There are people who have the ability, capability, and potential to do stupendous things in life. The challenge is that one has to be disciplined enough to do the work that is required to pull off the dream.

Sometimes the work involves getting up early to exercise if your dream is to lose weight or curtailing your diet by getting rid of the items that are causing the weight gain. Perhaps the dream is to attend college or a vocational program. The action requires contacting the educational institution for an application, paying the application fee, and finally submitting the application. The work may involve working long hours to obtain money to attend school or the police academy. The action may necessitate working during the day while attending college or vocational school at night to receive a long-awaited degree or certification. The work may involve sacrificing and saving money in order to launch a new business. The action may mean that you need to move to an area that has opportunities in the field of the job you have dreamt about for years. The action may mean eliminating the people in your life who are barriers, hindrances, and obstacles to helping you fulfill your dream. Action may require changing your location and vocation. Whatever action you must take to pull off your dream, do it!

I implore you to stop lamenting, pondering, stalling, and conjuring up excuses to prevent you from attaining your aspirations, dreams, and goals. I encourage to you to immediately act to pull off your dream in three simple words—just do it!

The most alarming and troubling issue that I face is encountering people who cast aside or abort their dreams because they have a fear (false evidence appearing real) of failure, lack self-confidence, or allow naysayers to stop them from taking action to produce their hopes and dreams. I encourage you not to have fear, be faint-hearted, have cold feet, or be rattled by the work that is involved to attain your dreams.

You have the God-given wisdom, gifts, and talents to act upon your dreams. God will grant you the fortitude, intellect, power, strength, stamina, and resources to accomplish the dream that has been deposited and planted in you.

I am mesmerized by a television show that offers entrepreneurship opportunities to dream bearers who have a product to promote.

The dream bearers have taken action by registering to participate in a television show that may lead to them fulfilling their dreams to become entrepreneurs.

The dream bearers have the arduous task of convincing several brutal and ferocious investors to invest in their product. Once the dreamers are able to encourage, persuade, and sway one of the investors to sow funding and entrepreneurial support for their product, the dreamers are flooded and overtaken with emotions.

The dream bearers have generally invested a lot of blood, sweat, tears, and money in their product. Some people have borrowed money from financial institutions, family and friends, and taken out a second mortgage and quit their jobs to work long hours on developing their product. They are overjoyed when they are able to realize their dreams. Their action by way of effort, toil, labor and struggle is what they needed to pull off their dreams.

The cosmetologist I referenced earlier had a desire to open her own business for seventeen years before she acted upon her dream. She had taken all of the business-related classes to become a competent and proficient entrepreneur. She acted upon and pulled off her dream when she consulted with a real estate agent to locate a building for her business. She met with the real estate agent and zeroed in on the facility that suited her dream. She already had a mental image of the building because she had clung to the dream for years. She signed the lease agreement and moved into the facility. She and her husband installed the appliances, equipment, and furniture in her new hair salon.

My cosmetologist currently has her own lucrative and thriving business because she relentlessly acted upon her dream. She did the work and, as a result, her dream came to fruition.

I mentioned that I had a life-changing event that could have caused me to nullify my dream. I decided several years after high school to activate my dream to receive my associate's degree and bachelor's degree. I had deliberated and dwelled on my dream to receive my college degrees long enough. It was time for me to take action if I was ever going to witness the manifestation of my dream!

Fortunately, I was married to an extraordinary and remarkable man who supported my dream. My husband in concert with my parents, siblings, and friends were staunch and unwavering cheerleaders! As I previously mentioned, I attained my associate's degree and bachelor's degree several years after I completed high school.

However, I was deeply inspired and emboldened by the college experience. I was so revitalized after I received my bachelor's degree, that I decided to engrave a goal in my journal that I initially believed was unattainable. I decided to pursue a master's degree! At the time, I had a full-time job as an elementary school teacher. I decided to attend college courses at night all while being a wife and mother. I was so profoundly inspired by my professors that I was on a relentless pursuit to attain a master's degree. Two years after I enrolled at the university, I received my master's degree. One would have thought that I would have stopped dreaming. After all, I had accomplished the deferred and delayed dream to attain my bachelor's degree. Surprisingly, I decided that I wanted to embark upon a second master's degree! I know it sounds bizarre but I received a second master's degree two years later. I could not stop dreaming! I had a bachelor's and two masters' degrees. One would have thought any sane person would have stopped there but I decided to enroll in a doctoral program. Some would have thought that my dream was laughable and quite frankly unaffordable! I had a talk with my husband, children, and parents. They all encouraged me to diligently pursue my dream. Five years after I enrolled at the university, I received my doctoral degree at a phenomenal and well-known university in Pennsylvania. I literally had to commit to driving to Pennsylvania twice a week for five years. Most people outside of my inner circle thought I was of an unsound mind!

It is time to stop contemplating and brooding over your dream! It is time to take the essential action to pull off your dream.

Your daily deeds should reflect that you are moving towards achieving your goals. You have to act by administering incremental steps to help you achieve your dreams. If you do the work that is required of you, your dreams will come to fruition and flourish and thrive.

Imagine if you had a trip on your bucket list to go to Italy. I prefer the term adventure list but in any event, your desire is to go to Italy. You have told every person you encountered along the expedition that one day your dream was to go to Italy. You completed your research about Italy. You arranged to receive your passport, you have researched the cost of the flight, hotel, and the average cost of food in Italy. You visited the travel agency, collected all of the brochures, and sought vacation time from your employer to visit Italy. The only thing left for you to do to pull off your dream was to pay for the trip. You realized that you had to act by saving your money if you wanted your dream vacation to come to fruition. Unfortunately, you had decided to spend your money on other things. You could not stop shopping and purchasing items that you really didn't need. You couldn't take the essential action to save the money required for you to visit

Italy. You still believed you were eventually going to Italy. The only way you would ever get to Italy was if someone was gracious enough to give you an all-expense paid trip to Italy, or if you won a trip to Italy on a game show! The point is that you must take action if you want to fulfill your dream to visit Italy. You must religiously do your work!

Action is required to fulfill your hopes and dreams! Pull off your dream by doing the work that is required of you to actualize your dream! Once you take the action to attain your dreams, you must insulate yourself with the right people!

CHAPTER FIVE

Insulate Yourself with the Right People to Pull Off Your Dream!

There are multitudes of gloomy people who encourage folks to call off and terminate their dreams. They are the people who constantly and habitually offer pessimistic responses whenever a person shares their hopes and dreams. We all know who they are because they have a negative outlook on life. The dull, murky, and down-in-the-dumps people are lurking around ready to place an overcast opinion about your dream! The ominous and miserable people are standing by with a fire extinguisher ready to douse and smother your dreams!

Most of the people who want to quench your dreams have not accomplished any goals, so therefore they don't want you to achieve anything worthwhile. They are the people who are settled and satisfied with their humdrum and insipid lives. As soon as one embarks upon a conversation about leaving a menial job to pursue a lucrative employment opportunity, the naysayer starts to share all of the risks associated with leaving the low-paying job. Any discourse about enrolling in college the skeptic starts to remind you of your age, vocation, and inability to afford the college courses.

You know who the gloomy family, friends, colleagues and peers are who are adamant about extinguishing and sabotaging your dreams. They are determined to discourage, dissuade, and hold you back from pulling off your dreams.

If you are on a zealous pursuit to attain and pull off your dream, you must remove the cheerless and dismal Debbie and Donald Downers in your life. Debbie and Donald Downers will serve as killjoys and prophets of doom in your life. They will be cynical and discourage you before you are able to pull off your dream.

Unfortunately, some of the people (dream killers) who consistently cast doubt and gloom upon you can be in your inner circle. They can be your parents, siblings, spouses, relatives, friends, teachers, counselors, etc. You have to strategically cushion and insulate yourself with positive people who want to observe you basking in all of the rich blessings that God has in store for you!

It is necessary to isolate yourself from people who have been strategically positioned in your life to assassinate your dreams and goals. You have to sequester yourself from the people who interfere and obstruct your ability to attain your goals. If you are going to pull off your dream, identify who the naysayers are and isolate and separate yourself from them!

I mentioned that my husband and family members were my cheerleaders. I am blessed that I have a testimony of a supportive family and friends while I worked on several college degrees. I ardently realize upon speaking to students that not everyone has the account that I have of a committed and devoted family and host of friends who were faithful in their pursuit to assist me as I accomplished my dreams.

Insulate yourself and link up with the genuine, idealistic, and merry people who will enable you to fulfill your hopes and dreams. The confident and uplifting people I am referencing may not be in your inner circle. However, cling and cleave to anyone you meet along the journey who offers you encouragement and support. A stranger can offer you words of inspiration. A fellow student, colleague, counselor, teacher, peer or pastor can be the person strategically positioned in your life to offer you the assistance you will need to accomplish and pull off your dream.

Don't be discouraged if members of your family don't support your dream. There are people who have been strategically assigned and deployed by God to insulate you so that you will be able to fulfill your dreams. Insulate yourself with the right people and obtain OCD to acquire and pull off your dream!

CHAPTER SIX

You Must Have OCD If You Want to Pull Off
Your Hopes and Dreams!

There are scores of people who departed earth with their hopes and dreams submerged in their hearts. There are also individuals who dwell amongst us who are walking around with dreams that have not been birthed or unearthed because they lacked OCD. Anyone who wants to pull off their aspirations, hopes, goals and dreams must have OCD! Optimism, consistency, and discipline are essential, necessary, and required if you are committed and determined to pull off your dream.

I noticed at the beginning of every New Year we are inundated and saturated with commercials about weight loss. I also noticed that retail store managers would strategically move the athletic apparel, exercise mats, gloves, videos, and dumbbells to the front of the store.

I must admit that in the past, I have gotten consumed with taking the pledge to lose weight every New Year. A visit to a retail store and a glimpse of a Weight Watchers, Jenny Craig and Nutrisystem commercial, I was inclined to think about my dream to lose weight. I would yank out the exercise attire that was buried in my drawer. I dusted off my elliptical and planned to start my exercise routine and weight-loss program.

I generally started by fathoming how difficult it would be to lose weight. I started thinking about all of the foods that would be restricted from my diet. The more I thought about embarking upon a routine weight loss program and exercise program, I became extremely pessimistic. I started thinking about how difficult the task was going to be and how long it would take me to accomplish my dream to lose weight. I also started appraising the amount of time it would take me to lose the weight.

I envisioned myself being miserable without cake, chocolate, and chips! I commenced deliberations of how much time it would take me to work out on the elliptical. Upon evaluation of how difficult it would be to accomplish my dream to lose weight, I mulled over all of the reasons why my dream was unattainable and realized that losing weight and dropping a dress size was simply a pipe dream. My pessimistic and defeated attitude caused me to terminate my dream to lose weight.

Once, I had the right attitude to lose weight. I gave serious thought to losing weight. I happily pulled out the exercise gear and hopped on my elliptical. I exercised for thirty minutes several days a week. I felt absolutely great! I had the endurance and stamina to successfully acquire several miles on my elliptical. Unfortunately, my dream to lose weight was short-lived. It all started when I decided to change my routine. My exercise schedule originally was five days a week. The days dwindled to three days, to two days a week, to once a week.

Ultimately, I no longer adhered to a regimented exercise schedule. I suddenly stopped working out because I lacked a consistent exercise plan.

My dream to lose weight was annihilated because I did not have the optimism, consistency, and discipline that were warranted to experience weight loss. I lacked OCD, the essential behavior needed to accomplish my goal to lose weight. Absent OCD, it will be nearly impossible to attain and pull off your dream!

Oftentimes, we embark upon our dreams with defeat. We set about our dreams with a negative mindset. We must plunge into our dreams with a healthy mindset. We have to envision what our lives would be like if we attained our dreams.

Optimism is having a state of positive beliefs. We must breed a spirit of enthusiasm and exhilaration if we plan to successfully accomplish our dreams. If optimism is lacking or omitted from the equation, it will be extremely difficult to pull off our dreams.

The most difficult task I had to complete was a doctoral dissertation. I can recall being in

Florida at the Hard Rock Café merrily talking on a pay phone to my dissertation chair about a revision that he wanted me to make to one of my chapters. I carried my dissertation everywhere, even on vacations! I would wake up in the middle of the night because I thought of some research that should be included in my dissertation. I was determined that I was going to successfully attain my dream to receive my doctoral degree. I had a positive and upbeat attitude about submitting the final document that would sign, seal, and deliver my degree.

I consistently set aside time to work on my dissertation. I omitted myself from an abundance of extracurricular activities. I did not attend a lot of social events because I was driven to accomplish my goal.

I invariably met with my dissertation chair to discuss the tenets of my research. I was dependable and showed up for the meetings on schedule. I was extremely diligent and vigilant about adhering to the requirements needed for me to complete my dissertation.

Fortunately, there are countless people who have dreams to attain their doctoral degrees. However, if you check with any university, the staff will inform you that they have flocks of people who completed all of the compulsory coursework to receive doctoral degrees. Unfortunately, there are students who have an ABD status. ABD stands for All But Dissertation!

It is disheartening to know that a host of people are walking around with unfulfilled dreams to receive their doctoral degrees because they have not completed the final project. The students embody the intelligence, knowledge, skills, and wisdom because they successfully completed the coursework. It takes consistency and discipline to expend countless hours conducting research and committing the findings to a dissertation.

Anyone who is walking around with an ABD status has not fulfilled their dream to receive their doctoral degree. They will need OCD to cross the finish line!

I am standing on the sidelines cheering for all the people with an ABD status. Activate and pull off your dream by jumping back into the race. You deserve that degree. You have already invested a great deal of time and energy in the coursework. You also expended a humongous and whopping amount of money on your courses! Trust God to empower you with the optimism, consistency and discipline you need to complete the race! All you need to bear is OCD and your dream will come to manifestation!

Chapter Seven

A MANIFESTATION of Your Dream!

There is an organization called the M25 Initiative. I admire and laud M25 Initiative volunteers because of their untiring and unwavering support of the disenfranchised and displaced citizens in New Jersey.

The M25 Initiative is a 501c3 nonprofit organization working to end homelessness by assisting the homeless with permanent and supportive housing. The organization has helped numerous homeless people fulfill their hopes and dreams to have a permanent home. I applaud and commend all the volunteers and donors who have made it possible to move homeless people from the streets or shelters to a permanent home! The volunteers and donors' acts of kindness and generosity is admirable, praiseworthy, and meritorious.

I have closely observed the work of the M25 Initiative. I have viewed the video-recorded testimonies of the homeless people who transitioned from the streets or living in cars for several years to a permanent home. The M25 Initiative team actually celebrates the new tenant by throwing a welcome-home party! The homeless people are often interviewed at the welcome-home party. The new residents are elated to declare and proclaim to have a home is a dream that has come to manifestation! A dream comes to manifestation when it is demonstrated, fulfilled, evident, disclosed, revealed, and materializes in a person's life!

The M25 Initiative was a dream that emanated and flowed in the heart of a local pastor who wanted to broaden the Code Blue Coalition to abate chronic homelessness. The pastor in concert with the local mayor and a team of community members reached for their goal to obliterate homelessness by embracing and mobilizing faith-based institutions, businesses, non-profit organizations, volunteers, donors, and politicians to assist them with pulling off their dream to abolish homelessness in the county.

The pastor did not mull over his decision to form the M25 Initiative to blot out homelessness. He acted by forming a team of committed and devoted members who immediately worked closely and incessantly with him to accomplish the dream to transition homeless people from the streets to permanent housing.

The M25 Initiative emerged from a dream that was placed in the heart of a man. The Lord bestowed upon the pastor the wisdom, gifts, talents, skills, and linked him with the resources, faith-based groups, nonprofit and charitable organizations, donors, and faithful volunteers to carry out the dream to manifestation!

The pastor of the M25 Initiative realized his dream to attend to homelessness in his county. Homeless people in the county recognize that it is possible to transition from the streets to a permanent residence.

Once your dream is fulfilled and comes to manifestation, give thanks and praise to God for allowing you to pull off your dream! You must celebrate the fulfillment of your dream! It is a celebratory time when there is a manifestation of your dream!

My hairstylist's dream came to manifestation seventeen years later when she opened her fruitful and profitable hair salon. Her husband, children, parents, family, friends, and clients championed her to grab hold of and pull off her dream. My hairstylist celebrated the grand opening of her salon with a host of family and friends.

I watched my dreams manifest when I paraded across the stage at several universities to receive my college degrees. I could hear my family and friends cheering as my name was called!

In May of 2003, I graduated from a University in Pennsylvania with a doctoral degree! My husband was so ecstatic and excited that after my five years of intense doctoral studies, he secured a limousine to transport me, our children, my parents, siblings, and grandmother to the commencement ceremony. He also celebrated the manifestation of my dream the same day by hosting a party that included two hundred people who supported and sponsored me during my five-year journey!

My friend of over thirty-six years participated in a nursing pinning ceremony when she received her college degree to become a registered nurse. She also secured and pulled off her dream when she successfully passed her licensing examination to become a registered nurse. She celebrated the manifestation of her dream with her family and friends. She also celebrated the manifestation of her dream by taking a well-deserved vacation!

I am anxiously looking forward to my high school seniors pulling off and securing their dreams. I foresee and look forward to hearing astonishing, incredible, and remarkable stories about their challenges, life experiences, adverse events, adjourned and deferred dreams they encountered along their odyssey to pull off their dreams.

I will be there to edify, encourage, sponsor, support and uplift the students along the journey. I will remind them of the gifts, talents, and skills that God has endowed them with to fulfill their dreams. Most importantly, I will celebrate when their dreams come to manifestation!

It is my hope that you too will experience the manifestation of the dream that you have been bearing and holding in the essence of your heart. It is time for you to put your dream in motion so that you can celebrate the manifestation of your dream!

CHAPTER EIGHT

Set Your Dream in Motion to Pull Off Your Dream!

We all have dreams. We have dreams and goals that encompass a whole gamut and spectrum of areas. This book was birthed on a dream that literally emitted from a conversation I had with my high school seniors. I desperately wanted my high school seniors to be committed to pulling off their dreams ten years from the time they graduated from high school.

My high school students may alter, revise, adjust, and delay or defer their dreams or possibly take a detour along the journey, but the nexus of their dreams remains constant. Their dreams are to be successful productive citizens who have attained an education, lucrative career, house, car, family, physical and spiritual wellness, and the resources to take care of their families.

All my high school seniors expressed attainable aspirations, dreams, and goals. We also have accomplishable and achievable dreams and goals. We have to do our work if we are going to pull off our dreams.

God will deposit a desire in your heart that is congruent with His word. If He has planted the desire in you, He will give you everything you need for your dream to come to manifestation.

It is imperative to reach for your dream because your dream is accessible and reachable. Your dream is possible and securable. You must fervently and vigorously go after your dream with every fiber of your being.

Your dream must be embraced. As you navigate through the terrain called life experiences, or naysayers who want you to abort your dream, it is essential that you tightly grab hold of and cling to your dream. Life experiences, challenges, hurdles and obstacles can cause you to let go of your dream. Whatever you do, keep fueling your dream and latch on to your dream.

It will take action on your part if you want your dream to materialize. It is time to move from desiring, reaching, and embracing your dream to administering the action that will enable you to execute and pull off your dream.

You have to put your plan in motion. You have done your due diligence by conducting your research. You know what resources you need to accomplish the task. You assessed and evaluated the terrain. You have the endurance, vigor, vitality, and strength to fulfill your dream. You have to acquire OCD to assist you with pulling off your dream. I beseech and entreat you to stay the course until you experience the manifestation of your dream!

I implore you that while you have breath in your body, pull off the dream that God has embedded and implanted in your heart. You must be determined not to succumb to naysayers or life experiences that may catapult you into neglecting your dream.

I hope you are not going to be one of the people who Ms. Viola Davis talked about during her acceptance speech. You must have a devoted and burning desire and steadfast faith that you will *not* depart this earth with unfulfilled dreams. God has planned some extraordinary, remarkable and unparalleled goals, dreams and service for you to accomplish while on earth.

My dream for you is what I desired for my high school seniors. I want you to activate and pull off your dream! I plead and urge you to take action to fulfilling your dream today. You are equipped with everything you need for your dream to come to manifestation!

You recorded your dream. Share your dream with someone who will insulate you and serve as a cheerleader and sponsor along your quest to pull off your dream.

Your dream will come to manifestation if you do your work! Remember the three simple words I mentioned earlier. Just do it!

I have faith and hope that you will pull off your dream! You are more than a conqueror! Recall and recollect the acronym for the word "dream"–Dream, Reach, Embrace, Action, and Manifestation and your dream will come to fruition. *Pull Off Your Dream!*

"*May He grant your heart's desires and make all your plans succeed.*" Proverbs 20:4 (NLT)

Bibliography

Cohen, Anne. "Every Single Magical Word in Viola Davis' best Supporting Actress Acceptance Speech". Refinery 29 February 26, 2017

Scripture quotations marked (NLT) are taken from the Holy Bible, New Living Translation, Copyright 1996 by Tyndale Charitable Trust. All rights reserved.